SCIENCE Q&A

THE ANIMAL KINGDOM

Cavendish
Square

New York

Published in 2016 by Cavendish Square Publishing, LLC
243 5th Avenue, Suite 136, New York, NY 10016

© 2016 Brown Bear Books Ltd

First Edition

Website: cavendishsq.com

CPSIA Compliance Information: Batch #WS15CSQ

The animal kingdom / edited by Tim Harris.
p. cm. — (Science Q&A)
Includes index.
ISBN 978-1-50260-619-8 (hardcover) ISBN 978-1-50260-618-1 (paperback)
ISBN 978-1-50260-620-4 (ebook)
1. Zoology — Juvenile literature. 2. Animals — Juvenile literature. I. Harris, Tim (Ornithologist). II. Title.

QL49.H37 2016
590—d23

For Brown Bear Books Ltd:
Editors: Tracey Kelly, Dawn Titmus, Tim Harris
Designer: Mary Walsh
Design Manager: Keith Davis
Editorial Director: Lindsey Lowe
Children's Publisher: Anne O'Daly
Picture Manager: Sophie Mortimer

Picture Credits:
T=Top, C=Center, B=Bottom, L=Left, R=Right

Front Cover : All pictures Shutterstock/Thinkstock.
Inside: Alamy: cbimages 26cr; Didier Descouens: 6tl; iStockphoto: 22tl, Natural Visions: Peter David 11tr; Shutterstock: 10b, Mark Beckwith 4, 26tl, Rich Carey 5br, 10tl, Hung Chung Chih 27tr, Dirk Ercken 1, 14tl, Chris Fourie 27l, Shane Gross 11bl, Claude Huot 22b, Gregory Johnston 19bc, Rich Lindie 7tr, Paul Wilkinson 10cr, Kim Worrell 23tl; Thinkstock: Ablestock 5tl, 18bl, Design Pics 14cr, Hemera 19tl, iStockphoto 6cr, 7bl, 15tr, 18tl, 18cr, 23tl, 26nl, Photos.com 14bl, Stockbyte 15bl.

Brown Bear Books has made every attempt to contact the copyright holder.
If you have any information please contact licensing@brownbearbooks.co.uk

Printed in the United States of America

CONTENTS

Introduction 4

Insects and Spiders 6

Insects and Spiders Q&A 8

Fish 10

Fish Q&A 12

Amphibians and Reptiles 14

Amphibians and Reptiles Q&A.... 16

Birds 18

Birds Q&A 20

Sea Mammals 22

Sea Mammals Q&A 24

Land Mammals 26

Land Mammals Q&A 28

Glossary 30

Further Reading 31

Index 32

INTRODUCTION

Humans share the world with more than eight million animal species, many of which remain mysterious. From the myriad colorful creatures of the sea, to reptiles, amphibians, birds, mammals, and insects, Earth is rich in diversity.

Take a look around you—how many animals can you see living nearby? You may have a cat, dog, or guinea pig, which are domesticated animals. Perhaps you can see blue jays, cardinals, or hummingbirds flying outside, or minnows and frogs in a nearby pond. It's certain that you will encounter at least one insect during the day—a butterfly, bee, spider, or ants. But have you ever stopped to wonder how a bird flies or a fish swims? In these pages, you will find out amazing facts, such as the way many insects change body form in a process called metamorphosis, how some spiders can paralyze prey, and how bees live in colonies where each has a specialized job.

◀ The cheetah is the fastest land mammal in the world. It can run at speeds of up to 60 miles per hour (100 kilometers per hour).

◀ Hummingbirds such as this ruby-throated hummingbird are among the smallest bird species on Earth. They feed on nectar from flowers.

You'll learn about the biology of different kinds of fish and how they form an important source of food for humans and other species. Amphibians such as frogs, toads, and salamanders spend part of their life in water and part on land. Follow a frog's journey from a tadpole swimming in a pond to an adult leaping on land, and learn about reptiles such as the Galápagos tortoise, which can live for over one hundred years and weigh up to 880 pounds (400 kilograms).

Discover awesome facts about birds, from the tiny bee hummingbird to the massive albatross and "talking" parrot. Finally, learn about our fellow mammals: From sea creatures like dolphins, whales, or manatees to land mammals such as lions, tigers, apes, and bears, humans share certain features with them all.

▶ The oceans are full of colorful species of fish, such as these schooling bannerfish and lyretail anthias in tropical waters.

INSECTS AND SPIDERS

Insects form the largest group of invertebrates. They include butterflies and moths, dragonflies, bees and wasps, beetles, and ants. Spiders are also invertebrates, but they are arachnids, not insects.

KEY FACTS

Species of insects: Over one million

Fastest insects: Dragonflies, 34 mph (55 kmh)

Species of spiders: At least thirty-four thousand

Most venomous spiders: Black widow and Brazilian wandering spider

▲ An adult dragonfly emerges from its dried-out larval case.

Adult insects have an external skeleton and a body that is divided into three parts: a head, thorax, and abdomen. On the head, they have two antennae and eyes made up of many separate sections (called compound eyes). Three pairs of legs are attached to the body. Most adult insects can fly. The oldest-known fossil insect is four hundred million years old.

Metamorphosis

Many insects change body form dramatically as they get older. This is called metamorphosis. For instance, butterflies and moths start life as eggs, which hatch into flightless, very hungry caterpillars. These grow larger before entering an inactive pupal stage. Inside the pupa, the insect undergoes a complete change, or metamorphosis, and emerges as a flying adult.

Dragonfly eggs hatch into swimming larvae that live in water. They may live underwater for several years before crawling out and emerging as flying adults.

GOLIATH INSECTS

The world's biggest insect is probably one of the goliath beetles, which live in tropical forests in Africa. Adults are up to 4.7 inches (12 centimeters) long and weigh up to 3.9 ounces (110 grams). They eat sugary tree sap and fruit. The world's biggest spider is the goliath tarantula, whose legs span 10 inches (25 cm). It sometimes eats small lizards and birds.

Social Creatures

Many bees, wasps, ants, and termites live in well-organized colonies, where different groups perform different tasks. Some build nests, guard eggs, and provide food for their young. Some ants protect other insects called aphids, so they can feed on a liquid called honeydew, which aphids produce.

Spiders

There are at least thirty-four thousand species of spiders, and they are all carnivores. Spiders have an external skeleton, or cuticle, and two body sections. The prosoma has the brain, eyes, and mouthparts. The stomach, reproductive organs, and lungs are in the opisthosoma. Four pairs of legs, a pair of fangs with poison glands, and a pair of grasping feelers attach to the prosoma.

Spiders often build webs in which to trap insect (or larger) prey. Spiders have special glands to produce the light, strong silk threads needed to make webs and nests. Prey such as flies get trapped

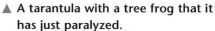

▲ **A tarantula with a tree frog that it has just paralyzed.**

in the webs. Other spiders hunt their prey on the ground. Most spiders use venom to kill or paralyze their prey. Only rarely is the venom dangerous to humans.

GENERAL INFORMATION

- In insects that undergo metamorphosis, the young and adult insects eat different sources of food. That means there is less competition between the different generations.

- One strand of spider silk long enough to circle Earth would weigh just 18 ounces (500 g).

- Like spiders, scorpions are arachnids.

▲ **These bees are swarming around the outside of their hive.**

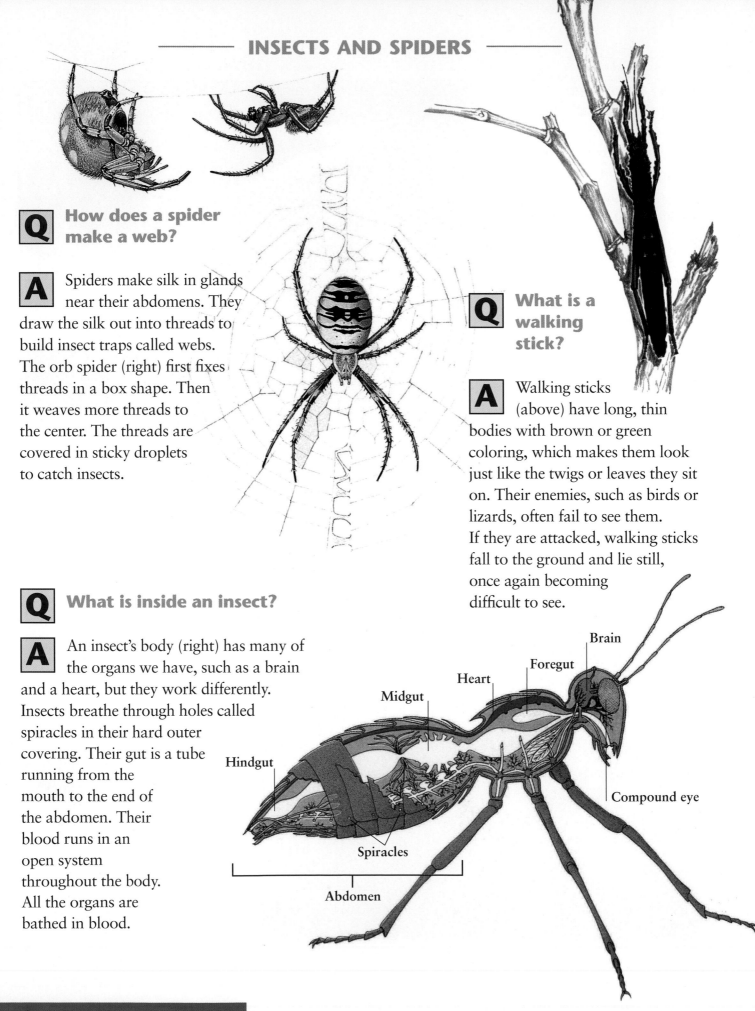

Q How does a spider make a web?

A Spiders make silk in glands near their abdomens. They draw the silk out into threads to build insect traps called webs. The orb spider (right) first fixes threads in a box shape. Then it weaves more threads to the center. The threads are covered in sticky droplets to catch insects.

Q What is a walking stick?

A Walking sticks (above) have long, thin bodies with brown or green coloring, which makes them look just like the twigs or leaves they sit on. Their enemies, such as birds or lizards, often fail to see them. If they are attacked, walking sticks fall to the ground and lie still, once again becoming difficult to see.

Q What is inside an insect?

A An insect's body (right) has many of the organs we have, such as a brain and a heart, but they work differently. Insects breathe through holes called spiracles in their hard outer covering. Their gut is a tube running from the mouth to the end of the abdomen. Their blood runs in an open system throughout the body. All the organs are bathed in blood.

Brain

Foregut

Heart

Midgut

Hindgut

Compound eye

Spiracles

Abdomen

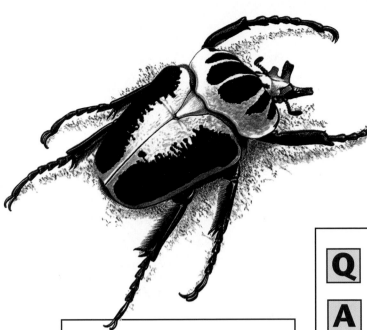

Q Which is the heaviest insect?

A The African goliath beetle (left) is the heaviest insect. It is as long as 4.7 inches (12 cm) and weighs up to 3.9 ounces (110 g). The lightest insect is the parasitic wasp the fairy fly, which is less than 0.008 inches (0.2 millimeters) long and weighs just 0.0002 ounces (0.006 g).

Q What do bees and wasps eat?

A Bees eat pollen and nectar, which they collect from plants and store in their nests, then turn into honey. Wasps kill other insects as food for their young.

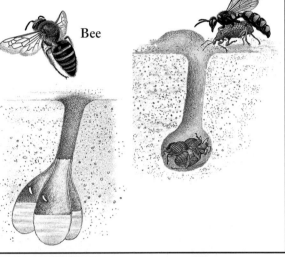

Bee

Wasp

Q How do grasshoppers "sing"?

A Grasshoppers make sounds by rubbing small pegs on their hind legs against a hard vein on their forewings. Males "sing" to attract a mate.

1. Eggs

2. Caterpillar (larva)

3. Pupa (chrysalis)

4. Adult butterflies

Q How does a butterfly begin its life?

A A butterfly begins life as an egg on a leaf. Out of the egg comes a tiny caterpillar (or larva), which eats the leaf and grows very fast. The caterpillar grows a hard covering and turns into a pupa (or chrysalis). After several days, or even weeks, the pupa case splits open and the butterfly crawls out. As soon as its wings have dried, it can fly away (right).

FISH

Fish live in water and use gills, rather than lungs, to breathe. They swim in all the world's oceans, freshwater lakes, and rivers, apart from those that are too polluted to support life.

▼ **Fish swim around a coral reef in the Red Sea.**

Most living fish have jaws, but the earliest fish did not. The first fish also probably had something called a notochord, made of cartilage, rather than a backbone. In all living fish apart from hagfish, the notochord that young fish possess develops into a backbone made of units called vertebrae.

What Makes a Fish?

Fish gain their warmth from the environment around them (they are ectothermic, or cold-blooded). They have a streamlined shape for swimming swiftly and have several

▲ **A salmon leaps up a waterfall to reach its spawning grounds.**

fins to help them change direction in the water. Most fish have skin that is covered with scales. Instead of breathing through internal lungs,

they have gills on the side of the head, which extract oxygen from the water. Fish have good senses. Most have sensitive receptors that form a lateral line system along each side. This system detects vibrations of other swimming animals.

Types of Fish

There are at least thirty-two thousand different kinds of fish, and they range in size from the whale shark, which is 52 feet (16 meters) long, to the stout infantfish, which grows to just 0.3 inches (8 mm).

Most fish live in the layer of water just below the surface (called the photic zone), but some thrive at great depths and in total darkness. In 2008, scientists investigating the ocean floor near Japan found a shoal of snailfish 25,260 feet (7,700 m) below the surface.

Some fish, including most of the sharks, are fearsome predators. The shortfin mako shark is capable of

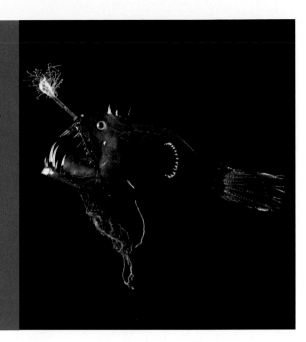

BIOLUMINESCENCE
Many fish that live in deep, dark ocean waters make their own light. They are bioluminescent. They use the light as a lure to attract prey. The anglerfish (right), for example, has a rod that dangles from its head with a bioluminescent light at the end. The light attracts prey, which the anglerfish then swallows.

swimming at 30 miles per hour (50 kmh) in pursuit of smaller fish, and the great white shark can kill prey as large as seals and dolphins.

Most fish lay, or spawn, eggs, from which small fish hatch. Female cod may produce four million eggs at once. However, the young develop inside the parent in some species; this is called viviparity.

Commercial Fishing

Fish are an important source of food for people. Commercial fishing catches around 103 million tons (93 million metric tons) of fish each year. The bulk of this is made up of herring, sardines, anchovies, cod, hake, haddock, and tuna. In addition, 53 million tons (48 million t) are produced in fish farms.

GENERAL INFORMATION

● **The oldest fossil fish was found in China, in rocks of the Cambrian period. The fossil is about 530 million years old.**

● **A shoal of fish is a loosely organized group, whereas a school is a tightly organized group whose movements are synchronized.**

▲ **A whale shark feeds by sucking water and plankton food into its mouth.**

FISH

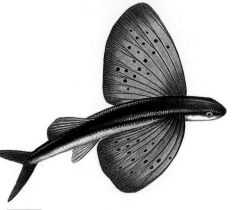

Q **What are the main parts of a fish?**

A The main parts on the outside of a fish are the gills (for breathing), the fins (for swimming and steering), and the lateral line (for detecting movement nearby).

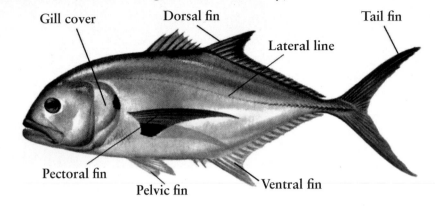

Gill cover

Dorsal fin

Tail fin

Lateral line

Pectoral fin

Pelvic fin

Ventral fin

Q **Can fish fly?**

A Flying fish (above) have large pectoral fins that act as wings. Their tails propel them out of the water to glide at speeds of 40 miles per hour (65 kmh).

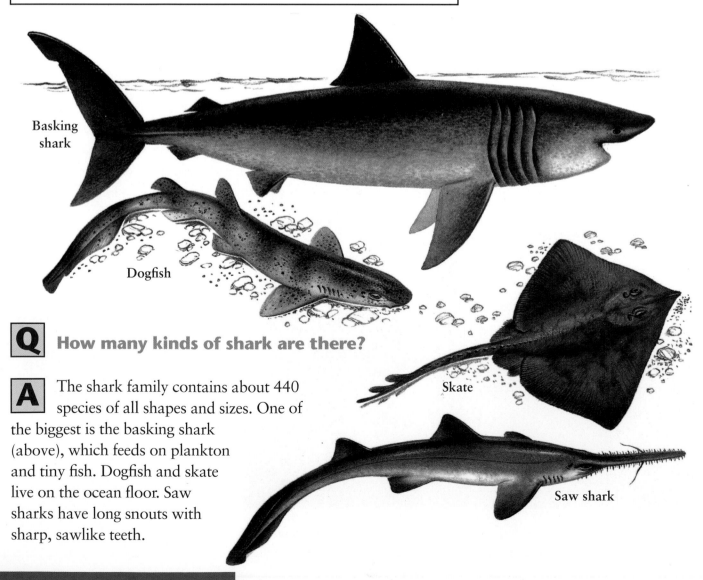

Basking shark

Dogfish

Skate

Saw shark

Q **How many kinds of shark are there?**

A The shark family contains about 440 species of all shapes and sizes. One of the biggest is the basking shark (above), which feeds on plankton and tiny fish. Dogfish and skate live on the ocean floor. Saw sharks have long snouts with sharp, sawlike teeth.

Q Which fish swims the fastest?

A Sailfish are the fastest swimmers, reaching speeds of up to 68 miles per hour (109 kmh). The fish's large dorsal fin lies flat against its body when swimming to help streamline it.

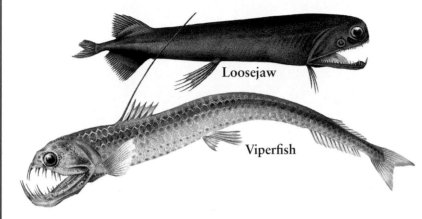

Loosejaw

Viperfish

Hatchetfish

Anglerfish

Q What lives at the bottom of the sea?

A It is very dark in the deep sea, but many strange fish and other creatures live there. The loosejaw has a huge gaping mouth that traps food. The viperfish is a fierce predator with long, sharp teeth. The hatchetfish has bulging eyes that help it see clearly in the gloom. The anglerfish attracts its prey by waving a shining lure on its snout.

Q Do all fish lay eggs?

A No. Several species, such as the sailfin molly (below), keep their eggs inside until they hatch. Then they give birth to as many as 140 live young.

Q How do cod find their food?

A Some species of fish, such as the Atlantic cod (below), have a single whiskerlike projection on their chins to help them feel for their food. This is called a barbel.

AMPHIBIANS AND REPTILES

Amphibians and reptiles are two groups of ectothermic ("cold-blooded") vertebrate animals. There are lots of similarities between the groups.

KEY FACTS

Number of amphibian species:
6,922 in 2012

Largest amphibian: Chinese giant salamander, up to 5.9 feet (1.8 m) long

Smallest amphibian: Many frogs grow to only 0.4 inch (1 cm) long.

Number of reptile species:
9,547 in 2012

Largest reptile: Saltwater crocodile, up to 20.7 feet (6.3 m) long

Smallest reptile: Dwarf gecko, just 0.6 inch (1.6 cm) long

▲ Tiger salamanders live mostly in burrows, only returning to water to breed.

▲ Jackson's chameleon is a reptile that lives in Africa. Only males have three horns on the head.

Frogs, toads, and salamanders are all amphibians. Most have four limbs when they are adults (the exceptions are wormlike creatures called caecilians). Typically, amphibians spend part of their life in water and part on land. Most undergo a dramatic body change from aquatic larvae that breathe with gills to air-breathing adults. This is called metamorphosis.

Frogs and toads start life as eggs, which hatch into limbless tadpoles. Tadpoles grow limbs and lose their tail as they get bigger, eventually changing into froglets or toadlets. Not all amphibians undergo metamorphosis; one example is the

TOADS IN THE DESERT

Amphibians live in all land environments, apart from places that are cold throughout the year. Some survive in dry deserts, but they have to make use of any water source very quickly. In the Mojave Desert in Southern California, red-spotted toads live underground for months at a time. They live off water stored in their large bladder. When rain falls, the toads hear the raindrops on the ground above. They dig their way to the surface, drink from a puddle, and look for a mate.

Mexican axolotl. Most amphibians can breathe through their skin as well as through lungs or (in larvae) gills. Some adult salamanders do not have lungs and breathe only through their skin.

Reptiles

Reptiles include crocodiles, snakes, lizards, and turtles. They live in a broad range of environments, from deserts to tropical rain forests. Many live in rivers and lakes, and others live in the ocean. Some, like crocodiles, alligators, and constrictor snakes, are fearsome predators, capable of tackling and killing large prey. Others, including many snakes, are not large but can subdue their prey with lethal injections of venom. However, most snakes are relatively harmless.

Most reptiles lay eggs, though these can survive out of water, unlike those of amphibians. Some reptiles give birth to live young. Unlike amphibians, reptiles do not have an aquatic larval stage.

▲ Galápagos tortoises live in the wild only on the Galápagos Islands, Ecuador. They can live to over one hundred years and weigh 880 pounds (400 kg).

GENERAL INFORMATION

- Amphibians evolved from lobe-finned fish in the Devonian period about 360 million years ago.

- Reptiles evolved between 320 and 310 million years ago, in the Carboniferous period; their ancestors were reptilelike amphibians.

- Dinosaurs were a group of reptiles that became extinct sixty-five million years ago.

▲ The Indian cobra has a distinctive hood on its head and sometimes grows to more than 6.5 feet (2 m) long. It paralyzes its prey with powerful venom.

Q **Where do cobras live?**

A The Indian cobra lives in southern Asia. When threatened, it spreads the ribs in its neck, forming a hood. This makes it appear bigger and frightens its enemy. The ringhals is an African cobra. The coral snake, which belongs to the cobra family, lives in American forests.

Indian cobra

Ringhals

Coral snake

Q **How can a chameleon look in two places at once?**

A A chameleon can swivel its eyes separately. One may be looking forward and the other backward. The eyes can also work together to focus on the same object.

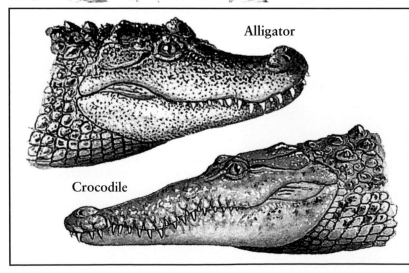

Alligator

Crocodile

Q **How can you tell the difference between an alligator and a crocodile?**

A When a crocodile closes its mouth, the fourth tooth in the lower jaw sticks up outside the top jaw. When an alligator does the same thing, this tooth is hidden.

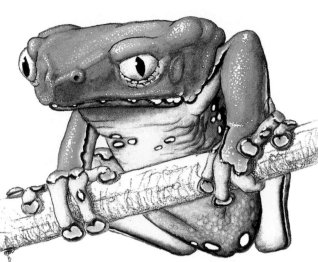

Q How do frogs climb trees?

A The tree frog (left) has round disks at the end of its toes. These act as suckers and help the frog climb up smooth leaves. The toes are long and can curl around thin twigs. Some tree frogs have sticky webbing between their fingers and toes that enables them to hold on more easily. The frog's belly skin is loose, and this also clings to the tree.

Q Why do reptiles flick out their tongues?

A This monitor lizard (right) is flicking out its tongue. Sometimes the tongue touches the ground, and sometimes it waves in the air. The tongue collects tiny chemical traces and takes them back to the mouth where nerve cells figure out what the chemicals mean. By doing this, the monitor can pick up signals about food and dangers nearby. Many lizards and snakes use their tongues in the same way.

Q How do frogs jump?

A A frog hops and leaps in just the same way as it swims. It lifts its front legs off the ground and pushes off with its powerful back legs (left). The pressure forces open the large webbed feet, giving the frog a firm base from which to jump. It lands on its front legs and chest, and then it gathers in its back legs, ready for another leap.

BIRDS

Birds are a large group of vertebrate animals. They live on every continent, including Antarctica, and on islands in every ocean. Most can fly, and all have feathers and lay eggs from which the young hatch.

KEY FACTS

Number of species: About ten thousand

Largest: Ostrich, 9 feet (2.75 m) tall

Smallest: Bee hummingbird, 2 inches (5 cm) long

Most common: Domesticated chicken (reared from wild red jungle fowl), twenty-four billion

Birds create their own body heat—they are endothermic (warm-blooded), unlike fish, amphibians, and reptiles. Their front limbs have evolved into wings, although not all birds fly.

All birds have a covering of feathers; these are sometimes brightly colored and used in courtship displays. Birds walk or run on their back limbs. Most birds grasp food with their bill, or beak.

▲ In the breeding season, many birds molt into bold new plumage, like this male mandarin duck.

The Power of Flight

Peregrine falcons are the fastest animals on Earth: they can fly at up to 200 miles per hour (325 kmh) when diving on their prey. And ostriches can run at 43 miles per hour (70 kmh). Many birds fly long distances at certain times of year to take advantage of changing food sources. This is called migration. For instance, Arctic terns raise their young around the Arctic Ocean but fly south in the fall to spend the next few months in the Southern Ocean. The record distance flown by an Arctic tern is 50,704 miles (81,600 km) in a single year. Some birds can hover, and hummingbirds can fly backward.

Penguins, ducks, gulls, and auks are very good swimmers. Gannets plunge into the water from great heights in pursuit of fish, and other species can dive to great depths.

◄ Ruby-throated hummingbirds weigh just 0.1 ounce (3 g). While hovering, their wings beat fifty-five times per second.

▲ Woodpeckers incubate their eggs and rear the young in a tree hole.

▶ Bald eagles are powerful birds of prey. They eat mostly fish.

Varied Diets

Owls, falcons, and eagles (birds of prey) eat other birds and mammals. Gannets and ospreys catch fish, and vultures feed on dead animals (carrion). Flycatchers and warblers eat mostly insects, while grouse, finches, and buntings have a diet of seeds and shoots. Parrots are particularly fond of fruit, and hummingbirds collect nectar from flowers. Birds' bills are adapted for eating their favorite foods. So, birds of prey have hooked beaks that can

tear flesh. Hummingbirds have long beaks that can reach inside flowers. And finches have stubby bills for crushing seeds.

INTELLIGENCE
Crows and parrots are some of the most intelligent animals. They can make and use tools. For instance, New Caledonian crows make stick probes of different shapes to pull insects from holes in trees. If a crow makes a probe that is particularly good, other crows nearby may learn to copy that shape.

Eggs and Chicks

After mating, adult females lay eggs, from which young birds (chicks) hatch. The number of eggs laid at any one time (a clutch) ranges from one to at least eighteen. They may be laid on the ground, on a cliff ledge, or in a specially constructed nest. The eggs are kept warm (incubated) by one or both parents while the young birds develop inside. Once they have hatched, the chicks are fed by one or both parents until they are able to fend for themselves. This may be before or after they are strong enough to fly.

GENERAL INFORMATION
● The ancestor of birds was probably similar to *Archaeopteryx*, fossils of which are found in Jurassic rocks in Germany. It has many birdlike features, but scientists are unsure if it was a bird or a dinosaur.

BIRDS

Q Which birds sleep in the air?

A Swifts (Alpine swift, below) sleep, feed, and even mate in the air. They are perfectly built for flying. Their long, swept-back wings help them fly fast and high in the sky, where they hunt for insects. But their legs and feet are weak. It is hard for swifts to hop or walk. Some swifts spend almost all their lives flying.

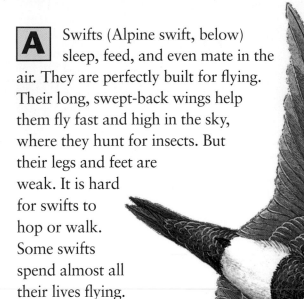

Q How can owls hunt in the dark?

A An owl (below) listens for the sounds of shrews or mice. It swivels its head until the sound is equally loud in both ears. The owl can then pinpoint exactly where the sound is coming from.

Q How do penguins keep their eggs warm?

A King penguins (right) live near the cold South Pole. The females each lay one egg on the ice in midwinter. The male penguin tucks the egg between his feet and his bulging stomach to keep it warm, until it hatches about two months later.

Q Why do parrots "talk"?

A In the wild, parrots are sociable birds, and they call to each other with clicks, squeaks, and screams. When they are kept in captivity, they sometimes seem to speak like humans. However, the parrots are not really speaking. They are just copying human voices.

Q How do hummingbirds feed?

A Hummingbirds, such as this sword-billed hummingbird, feed on insects and flowers. They poke their long, thin bills and long, tubelike tongues into the flower and suck up the nectar. To do this, the birds have to hover in midair. They can beat their wings up to seventy times every second. This makes the humming sound that gives the birds their name. Hummingbirds can also fly backward.

Q Which bird has the widest wingspan?

A Some species of albatrosses (below) have a 10-foot (3 m) wingspan—the longest of any bird. Albatrosses are sea birds that glide over the waves for hours. They ride on air currents, rarely flapping their long, narrow wings.

Q Why do birds have colorful feathers?

A Most brightly colored birds are males. Females of the same species may be duller. The males use their colors to attract a mate. Some species, such as the Raggiana bird of paradise (right), display their spectacular feathers by calling, jumping around, or even hanging upside down from a branch. The female's dull plumage helps her hide from danger when she is incubating the eggs.

SEA MAMMALS

Dolphins, whales, seals, and manatees spend their life in water. Seals come ashore to rest and breed, but dolphins and whales never come onto land.

The mammals that are most at home in the sea are dolphins and whales (collectively called cetaceans), manatees, and seals. The shape of their bodies helps them move easily through water. Their front limbs have evolved into flippers to help them maneuver.

Cetaceans

Cetaceans do not have fur to keep them warm, but they do have a thick layer of blubber beneath their skin to protect them from the cold. Both female dolphins and whales give birth to a single calf underwater.

Unlike fish, cetaceans such as porpoises and dolphins have lungs rather than gills, so they must come to the surface to breathe air. However, they can go long periods between taking breaths. Some species dive deep in search of food. For instance, a sperm whale may dive to 10,000 feet (3,000 m) when pursuing squid.

KEY FACTS

Cetaceans: About eighty-six species live in seas and oceans

Largest: Blue whale, 100 feet (30 m) long and 200 tons (180 t) in weight

Deepest diver: Sperm whale, 9,840 feet (3,000 m)

Seals and sea lions: Thirty-four species

▼ A humpback whale breaches, or leaps out of, the water.

◄ Sea otters eat mostly marine invertebrates, though some populations also eat lots of fish.

OTHER SEA MAMMALS

Other mammals spend long periods of time in seawater. The herbivorous manatees and dugongs spend their whole life in the warm waters of the Gulf of Mexico, and the Caribbean, Indian, and Pacific Oceans. Sea otters live in the cold waters of the northern Pacific Ocean, where they eat shellfish. Polar bears are excellent swimmers and fearsome predators, hunting and eating seals. One was tracked as she swam 427 miles (687 km) in nine days.

Some cetaceans have teeth and feed on fish and other marine animals. Others filter tiny animals called krill from seawater using baleen plates in their mouths.

"Talking" Underwater

Whales and dolphins have an excellent sense of hearing. They communicate information with groans, whistles, and clicks. Since they can hear very low-frequency sounds that have traveled through the water, they are able to keep in touch with other members of their species, even when they are far away. They also listen for the echoes of sounds they make when they are searching for food. Even in total darkness, they can tell whether an object is large or small and how far away it is; this is called echolocation.

Seals and Sea Lions

Seals and sea lions (in a group called pinnipeds) are superb swimmers.

▲ Walruses are pinnipeds with distinctive large tusks. They live in the cold Arctic Ocean.

Their limbs are short, flat, wide flippers, ideally suited for swimming. Like cetaceans, seals breathe air at the surface, but they can remain underwater for up to two hours on hunting expeditions.

They eat fish, shellfish, squid, and in the Southern Ocean, penguins. Some are furry, and all have a layer of insulating blubber.

Female seals and sea lions give birth to a single calf on land. In some species, males and several females form a family group.

The walrus is a very distinctive pinniped with two long tusks.

GENERAL INFORMATION

- Cetaceans are believed to have evolved from mammals that lived on land; they probably had the same ancestor as modern hippopotamuses.
- Scientists believe that pinnipeds evolved from a bearlike ancestor about twenty-three million years ago.

23

Q **What is the largest animal in the world?**

A The blue whale (below) is the largest animal that has ever lived on Earth. It can grow to 100 feet (30 m) long and weigh 200 tons (180 t).

Q **Which whale can dive the deepest?**

A The sperm whale (right) can dive to a depth of more than 10,000 feet (3,000 m). It goes down to the seabed in search of squid to eat. Sperm whales can spend an hour underwater before coming to the surface to breathe.

Q **Can polar bears swim?**

A Polar bears (above) are strong swimmers and can travel long distances in the icy waters of the Arctic. Their fur is thick and waterproof, and their feet are partly webbed.

Q **What is a dugong?**

A A dugong, or sea cow, is a mammal that lives in the warm waters of the southwest Pacific. It eats sea grasses, which it digs up from the shallows. It is a good swimmer, with a flat, forked tail.

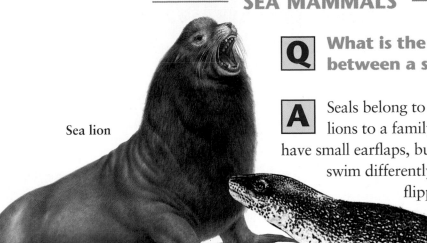

Sea lion

Seal

Q **What is the difference between a seal and a sea lion?**

A Seals belong to a family called true seals, and sea lions to a family called eared seals. Eared seals have small earflaps, but true seals have none. They also swim differently: eared seals mainly use their fore flippers, and true seals use their hind flippers.

Q **Do whales migrate in winter?**

A Yes. The northern bottlenose whale, for example (right), overwinters in the warm waters off the East African coast in the east and off of New York in the west. In the summer, it returns to the North Atlantic.

Q **Why do walruses have tusks?**

A The tusks of a walrus are the upper canine teeth, which grow very long, sometimes to 3 feet (1 m) in length. Male walruses (left) usually have longer tusks than females. Walruses use their tusks to scrape up the shellfish and clams that they eat, and for gripping the ice or fighting enemies. Their tusks are also the sign of a walrus's age and importance. The animal with the longest tusks leads the herd.

LAND MAMMALS

Mammals are vertebrate animals. All breathe air, make their own body heat (they are warm-blooded, or endothermic), and the females produce milk in mammary glands to feed their young.

KEY FACTS

Number of species: About 5,488

Largest: African elephant, up to 24 feet (7.3 m) long and 13 tons (12 t) in weight

Smallest: White-toothed shrew and bumblebee bat, 1.2–1.4 inches (3–3.5 cm) and 0.07 ounces (2 g)

Fastest: Cheetah, sprints at 60 mph (100 kmh)

▼ A young Thomson's gazelle suckles from its mother. This grazing species is very common on the dry grasslands of Kenya and Tanzania in Africa.

Mammals occupy almost every environment on Earth, from the equator to the shores of Antarctica. They live in waterless deserts, lush rain forests, baking-hot African grasslands, and icy tundra.

Most animals live on or close to the ground. Some dig burrows in which they sleep and raise their young. Often these animals leave their burrows only at night. Others, including monkeys, squirrels, sloths, and some rodents, spend much of their lives high in trees.

Some mammals can fly. The front limbs of bats have evolved over millions of years to form wings. Those bats that hunt at night have

▲ Microbats have large ears to pick up their echolocation calls.

another ability—echolocation. The animals make high-pitched calls that bounce off obstacles and flying insects, enabling them to find their way and hunt in near-total darkness.

Food

The variety of food that mammals eat is as varied as the animals themselves. Many graze, browse leaves, or pick fruit from trees. Others eat insects and other invertebrates. Some are carnivores, ambushing or pursuing other animals. And a small number of land mammals catch fish from riverbanks.

Raising the Young

Most kinds of mammals develop for a long time in their mother's womb before they are born. The placenta is the link between the parent and

the offspring during this period of gestation, or pregnancy. It ensures that nutrients and oxygen travel to the growing embryo and waste products flow the other way. The young are born as miniature versions of the adult. Placental mammals include elephants, cats, bears, and rabbits.

Mammals such as kangaroos are marsupials. The young develop inside the mother for a shorter time, and they are born much sooner. Then, young kangaroos crawl to the mother's pouch and drink milk from glands there until more fully grown. The gestation time of a kangaroo is brief: only four or five weeks.

GIANT PANDAS

Giant pandas are very rare mammals that live in China. One reason they are so rare is that they eat only bamboo in the wild, and the bamboo forests are shrinking. Pandas have to eat huge amounts of bamboo—20–30 pounds (9–14 kg) a day—because it is not very nutritious. Also, a panda has the digestive system of a meat-eating mammal, so the food is not digested efficiently.

▶ Adult male African elephants are the largest of all the land mammals. Females have the longest gestation period of any mammal—twenty-two months.

GENERAL INFORMATION

● Land mammals first appeared about 220 million years ago, in the Triassic period, although mammal-like animals appeared long before this time.

● Apart from placental and marsupial mammals, there is a third kind, the monotremes, which lay eggs. Echidnas and platypuses are monotremes.

LAND MAMMALS

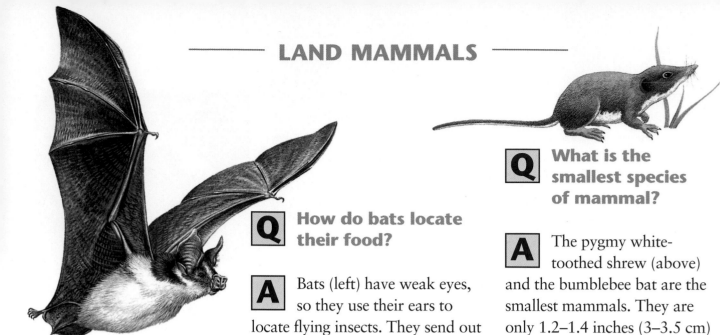

Q How do bats locate their food?

A Bats (left) have weak eyes, so they use their ears to locate flying insects. They send out high-pitched noises and listen for the echoes. They can tell if the echo comes from an insect, and they figure out exactly where it is.

Q What is the smallest species of mammal?

A The pygmy white-toothed shrew (above) and the bumblebee bat are the smallest mammals. They are only 1.2–1.4 inches (3–3.5 cm) long and weigh 0.07 ounces (2 g). Pygmy white-toothed shrews eat grasshoppers—which may be almost as big as they are.

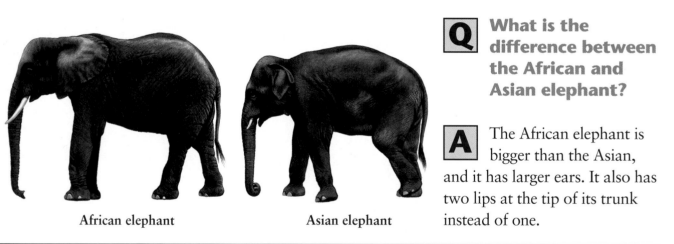

African elephant

Asian elephant

Q What is the difference between the African and Asian elephant?

A The African elephant is bigger than the Asian, and it has larger ears. It also has two lips at the tip of its trunk instead of one.

Q Which is the fastest mammal?

A The cheetah (right) can sprint in short bursts at a speed of 60 miles per hour (100 kmh), faster than any other land animal. It stalks its prey until it is very close, then breaks cover and runs in long, fast strides.

Q How does a camel survive in the desert?

A Camels (right) can go for weeks without drinking. They lose very little water from their sweat or urine. The camel's fur coat protects it from the heat of the sun, and it can close its nostrils to keep out sand and dust. Wide feet help it walk over soft sand without sinking. Despite popular belief, camels do not store water in their humps. The humps are used to store fat, which is used for food.

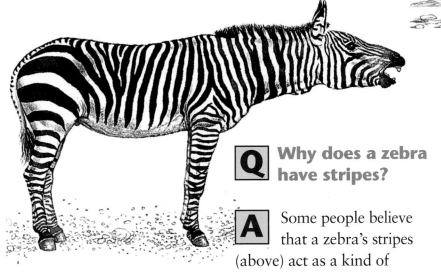

Q Why does a zebra have stripes?

A Some people believe that a zebra's stripes (above) act as a kind of camouflage, making individual animals hard to spot. But now scientists think there are other reasons for the stripes. They may dazzle lions and other cats that attack the zebra. Or they may help the members of a zebra herd recognize each other.

Q How can you tell a monkey from an ape?

Woolly monkey

A Monkeys and apes are both primates. Apes, such as the gorilla, have no tail. They have strong arms that are longer than their legs. Most monkeys, like the woolly monkey, have a tail with which they can hang from trees.

Gorilla

GLOSSARY

arachnid An invertebrate arthropod animal such as a scorpion, spider, or tick.

caecilian A wormlike amphibian that lives in the tropics, does not have limbs, and has poorly developed eyes.

carnivore An animal that eats flesh.

cetacean A marine mammal such as a dolphin, whale, or porpoise.

chrysalis The pupa stage in the life of a butterfly or moth.

echolocation Finding the location of something using reflected sound that is bounced back to the sender. Dolphins and bats both use echolocation.

ectothermic Describes an animal that depends on an outside source of heat—such as sunlight—to stay warm; a cold-blooded creature, such as fish, reptiles, and amphibians.

endothermic Describes an animal that makes heat within its body; a warm-blooded creature, such as a bear, cat, or bird.

gestation The process of being carried in the womb between conception and birth; the pregnancy term.

herbivore An animal that eats only plants and not flesh. Cows and manatees are herbivores.

invertebrate An animal without a backbone, such as a mollusk or worm. Invertebrates make up 95 percent of all animal species.

marsupial A mammal whose young are born not wholly developed and then suckled in a pouch on the mother's belly. Opossums and kangaroos are marsupials.

metamorphosis The process of changing from an immature to an adult form of animal, such as a tadpole turning into a frog.

monotreme A mammal that lays large eggs. The platypus and echidna are both monotremes.

paralyze To make something unable to move. Some venomous spiders and snakes are able to paralyze their prey.

pinniped A carnivorous mammal that lives in water, such as a walrus or a seal.

predator An animal that preys on other creatures for food.

venomous An animal that has venom or poison, such as certain types of snake.

vertebrate An animal with a backbone. Birds, fish, mammals including humans, amphibians, and reptiles are all vertebrates.

viviparity Giving birth to live young that develop inside the parent.

FURTHER READING

Books

Dorling Kindersley editors. *The Animal Book.* New York: Dorling Kindersley, 2013.

Honovich, Nancy, and Darlyne Murawski. *Ultimate Bugopedia: The Most Complete Bug Reference Ever.* Washington, DC: National Geographic Kids, 2013.

Hoyt, Erich. *Weird Sea Creatures.* Richmond Hill, ON: Firefly Books, 2013.

Spelman, Lucy. *National Geographic Animal Encyclopedia: 2,500 Animals with Photos, Maps, and More!* Washington, DC: National Geographic Children's Books, 2012.

TIME For Kids Magazine editors. *TIME For Kids Zoo 3D: An Incredible Animal Adventure.* New York: Time For Kids, 2012.

Websites

Animals: National Geographic Kids
kids.nationalgeographic.com/animals
Discover the world of your favorite animals, from orcas to orangutans, and find out fascinating facts about their food and habits. With breathtaking photos and an easy search engine by animal or habitat type.

Save the Manatee Club
www.savethemanatee.org
Find out all about the manatee, a large water mammal on the endangered list, and what people are doing to help save these intelligent creatures. Includes photos, underwater manatee cams, video footage, and audio of the manatee "language."

Smithsonian National Zoological Park
nationalzoo.si.edu/Animals
Learn about the biology, diet, behavior, and history of the 1,800 animals at the National Zoo, from bison and otter to great apes. Includes the Panda Cam, where you can watch rare giant pandas live online, plus photos of your favorite animals.

Publisher's note to educators and parents: Our editors have carefully reviewed these websites to ensure that they are suitable for students. Many websites change frequently, however, and we cannot guarantee that a site's future contents will continue to meet our high standards of quality and educational value. Be advised that students should be closely supervised whenever they access the Internet.

INDEX

A

African goliath beetle
 4, 9
albatrosses 5, 21
alligators 15–16
amphibians 4–5, 14–18,
 30
anglerfish 11, 13
Antarctica 18, 26
ants 4, 6–7
apes 4, 29
aphids 7
arachnids 6–7, 30
Archaeopteryx 19
Arctic 18, 23, 24,
Arctic tern 18
auks 18

B

bats 26, 28, 30
bears 5, 23–24, 27, 30
bees 4, 6–7, 9
beetles 4, 6, 9
bioluminescence 11
bird of paradise 21
birds 4–6, 8, 18–21, 30
blue whale 22, 24
butterflies 6, 9

C

caecilians 14, 30
camels 29
carnivores 7, 26, 30
cats 27, 29
cetaceans 22–23, 30

chameleons 14, 16
cheetahs 26, 28
chrysalis 9, 30
cobras 15–16
cod 11, 13
commercial fishing 11
crocodiles 14–16
crows 19

D

dolphins 5, 11, 22–23,
 30
dragonflies 6
ducks 18
dugongs 23–24

E

eagles 19
echolocation 23, 26, 30
ectothermic 10, 14, 30
elephants 26–28
endothermic 18, 26, 30

F

falcons 18–19
fish 4–5, 10–13, 15,
 18–19, 22–23, 26, 30
flycatchers 19
frogs 4–5, 7, 14, 17, 30

G

gannets 18–19
geckos 14
gestation 27, 30
giant pandas 27
grasshoppers 9, 28

gulls 18

H

herbivores 30
hummingbirds 4–5,
 18–19, 21

I–K

insects 4–9, 19–21, 26,
 28
invertebrates 6, 23, 26,
 30
kangaroos 27, 30

M

manatees 5, 22–23, 30
marsupials 27, 30
metamorphosis 4, 6–7,
 14, 30
microbats 26
migration 18
monkeys 26
monotremes 27, 30

O–P

owls 18–20
parrots 5, 19–20
penguins 18, 20, 23
photic zone 11
pinnipeds 23
plumage 18, 21
polar bears 23–24
porpoises 22, 30
predators 11, 13, 15, 23,
 30

R

rabbits 27
reptiles 4–5, 14–18, 30

S

salamanders 5, 14–15
salmon 10
sea lions 25
sea otters 23
seals 11, 22–23, 25, 30
sharks 10–12
shrews 20, 26, 28
spawning grounds 10
spiders 4, 6–8, 30
swifts 20

T

tarantula 6, 7
termites 7
toads 5, 14
tortoises 5, 15

V

vertebrates 6, 14, 18,
 23, 26, 30
viviparity 11, 30

W–Z

walking sticks 8
walruses 23
warblers 19
wasps 6–7, 9
whales 5, 22–25, 30
zebras 29